BOOK 3 - B♭ Clarinet

STANDARD OF EXCELLENCE

COMPREHENSIVE BAND METHOD

By Bruce Pearson

Dear Student:

Welcome to STANDARD OF EXCELLENCE Book 3.

By now, you have demonstrated that you are making steady progress toward becoming an accomplished musician. With the skills you are mastering on your instrument, you are beginning to realize the value of hard work and the joy of music-making.

STANDARD OF EXCELLENCE Book 3 introduces you to some of the world's finest music. By performing this literature, you will gain an appreciation for a variety of musical styles while improving your individual instrument and ensemble skills.

Best wishes as you explore Book 3.

Sincerely,

Bruce Pearson

Practicing - the key to EXCELLENCE!

▶ Make practicing part of your daily schedule. If you plan it as you do any other activity, you will find plenty of time for it.

▶ Try to practice in the same place every day. Choose a place where you can concentrate on making music. Start with a regular and familiar warm-up routine, including long tones and simple technical exercises. Like an athlete, you need to warm-up your mind and muscles before you begin performing.

▶ Set goals for every practice session. Keep track of your practice time and progress on the front cover Practice Journal.

▶ Practice the hard spots in your lesson assignments and band music over and over, until you can play them perfectly.

▶ At the end of each practice session, play something fun.

ISBN 0-8497-5978-1

KJOS NEIL A. KJOS MUSIC COMPANY, PUBLISHER

W23CL

REVIEW	C MAJOR KEY SIGNATURE	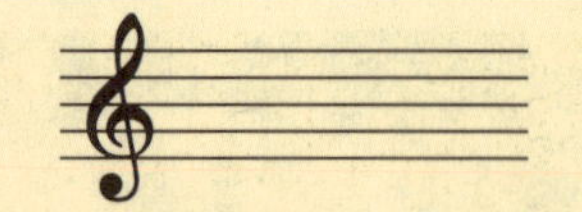
STYLE	*simile* - Continue playing in the same manner.	

1 WARM-UP - Band Arrangement

▶ Plan where to take breaths.

2 TECHNIQUE BREAK

▶ Try playing both octaves.

3 RIG A JIG JIG

American Folk Song

4 TECHNIQUE BREAK

▶ * Use the alternate F♯/G♭ fingering.

REVIEW

A MINOR KEY SIGNATURE

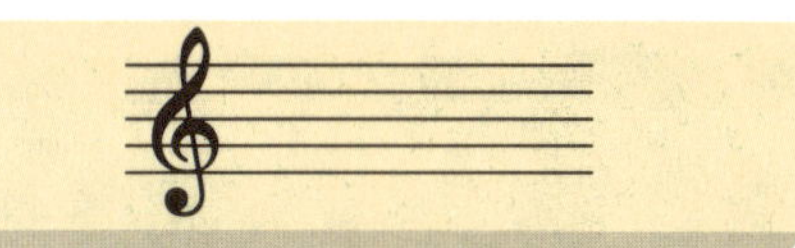

5 A MINOR SCALE SKILL (Concert G Minor)

▶ Try playing both octaves.

6 PAT-A-PAN

French Carol

7 INTERVAL INQUISITION

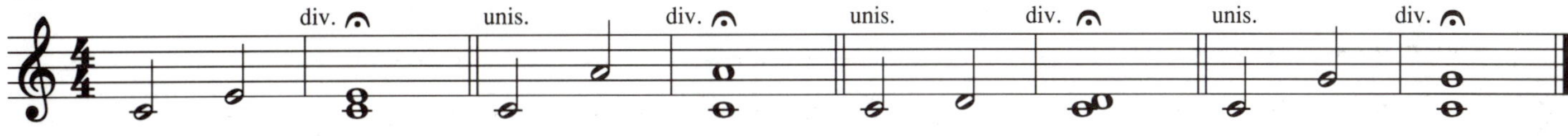

▶ Write in the intervals on the lines provided.

8 ARTICULATION ADVENTURE

9 GO FOR EXCELLENCE!

▶ Lines with a medal are *Achievement Lines*. The chart on the inside back cover can be used to record your progress.

REVIEW

F MAJOR KEY SIGNATURE

MAJOR CHORD

MINOR CHORD

DYNAMICS

fortissimo (ff) - very loud ***pianissimo (pp)*** - very soft

10 DYNAMIC DYNAMICS

11 MAJOR AND MINOR CHORD EAR TRAINER

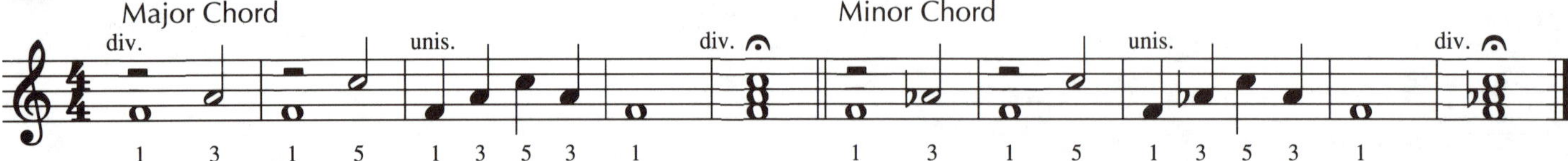

▶ Sing before you play.

12 TECHNIQUE BREAK

13 MY PARTNER AND I

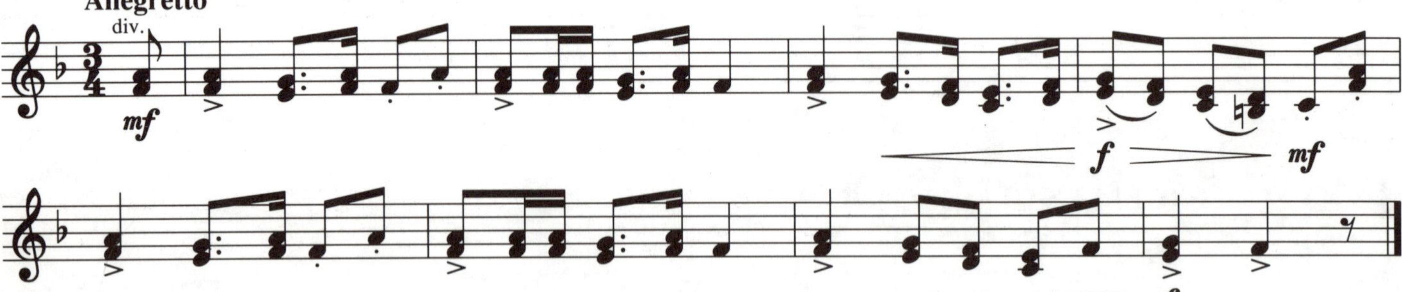

14 FOR CLARINETS ONLY

Page 44

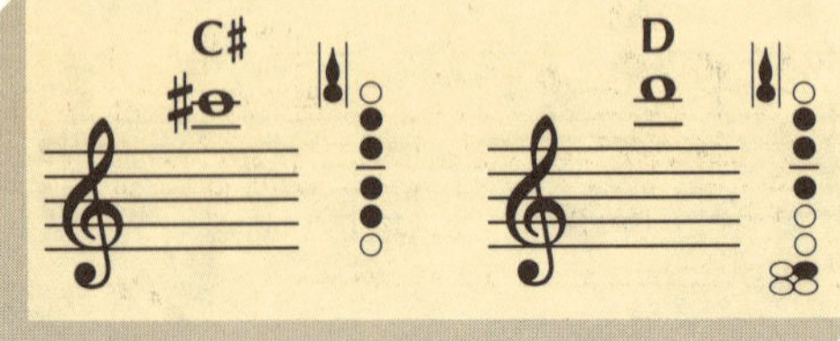

▶ When you see a page number followed by an arrow, *Excellerate* to the page indicated for additional studies.

REVIEW

D MINOR KEY SIGNATURE

ENHARMONICS

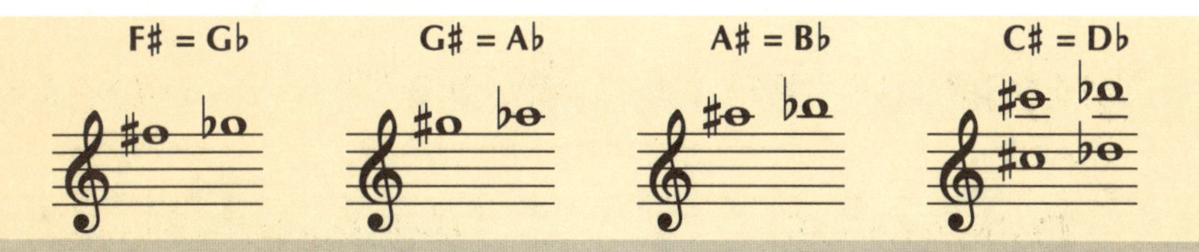

15 CHORALE - Band Arrangement

John B. Dykes (1823 - 1876)

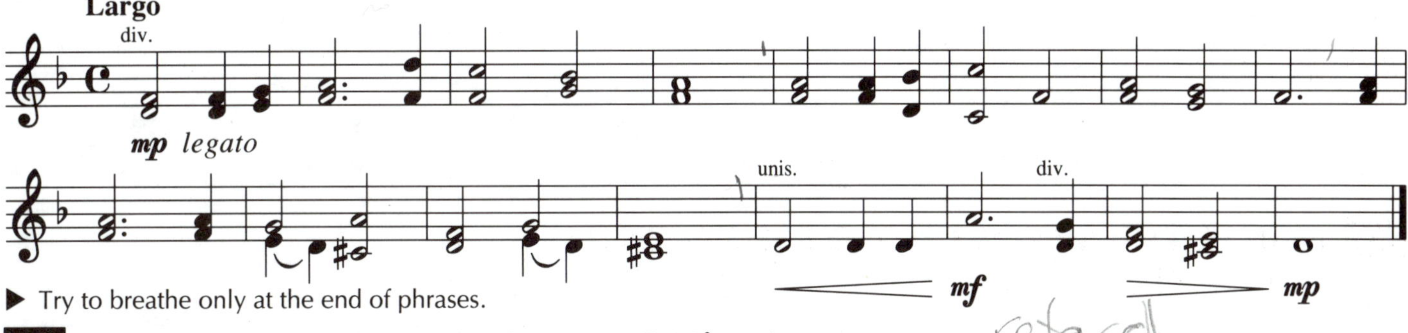

▶ Try to breathe only at the end of phrases.

16 D MINOR SCALE SKILL (Concert C Minor)

▶ Try playing both octaves.

17 TUMBALALAIKA

Jewish Folk Song

18 TECHNIQUE BREAK

19 GO FOR EXCELLENCE!

▶ * Use the alternate F♯/G♭ fingerings.
▶ Try playing both octaves.

REVIEW

G MAJOR
KEY SIGNATURE

20 WARM-UP - Band Arrangement

21 TECHNIQUE BREAK

▶ Try playing both octaves.

22 THE BRITISH GRENADIERS

English Folk Song

▶ Try to breathe only at the end of phrases.

23 FOR CLARINETS ONLY

▶ Keep your right hand down for these exercises.

REVIEW

D MAJOR KEY SIGNATURE

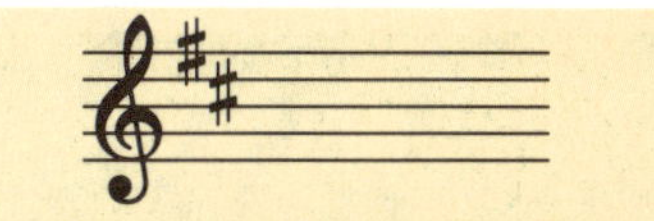

SIXTEENTH/ DOTTED EIGHTH NOTE COMBINATION

24 D MAJOR SCALE SKILL (Concert C Major)

Page 44

▶ Try playing both octaves.

25 ARTICULATION ADVENTURE

▶ Write in the counting for the top line before you play.

26 GREEN GROW THE RASHES O

Scottish Folk Song

27 TECHNIQUE BREAK

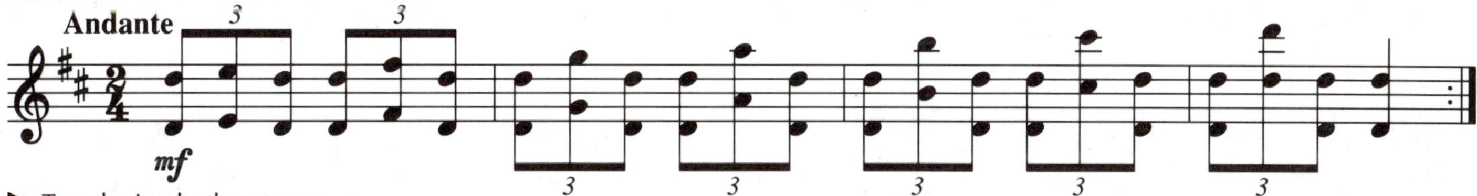

▶ Try playing both octaves.

28 GO FOR EXCELLENCE!

Scottish Folk Song

REVIEW

B♭ MAJOR KEY SIGNATURE

SIXTEENTH/EIGHTH/SIXTEENTH NOTE COMBINATION

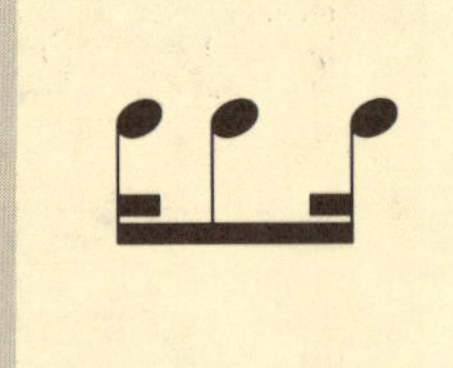

29 B♭ MAJOR SCALE SKILL (Concert A♭ Major)

Page 44

▶ Try playing both octaves.

30 ARTICULATION ADVENTURE

▶ Write in the counting for the top line before you play.

31 LA RASPA

Mexican Folk Song

32 TECHNIQUE BREAK

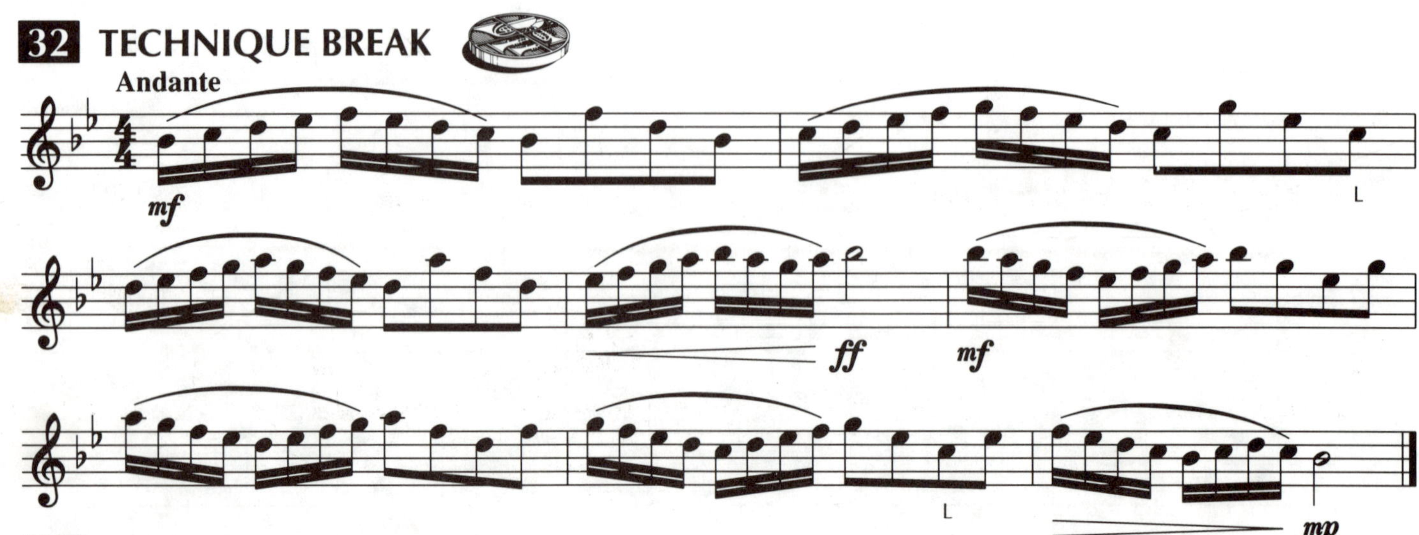

33 LONDONDERRY AIR - Band Arrangement
Irish Folk Song
arr. Bruce Pearson (b. 1942)
Andante
div.
mf legato f mf f mf
f mf rit. f p
34 TECHNIQUE BREAK
Andante
mf
35
Composer
your name
Compose a song that is shaped like the curved lines. Title and play your composition.
36 PENTATONIC SCALES
A
Andante
mp
B
Andante
mp
Pentatonic scales consist of five notes. Two forms of the pentatonic scale are shown above.
37 GO FOR EXCELLENCE!
Korean Folk Song
Andante
"Arirang"
3
mp pp
3
mf mp
"Arirang" is based on a pentatonic scale.

E MINOR KEY SIGNATURE

E minor has the same key signature as **G major**.

TEMPO

Andantino - Faster than **Andante**, but not as fast as **Moderato**.

ENHARMONICS

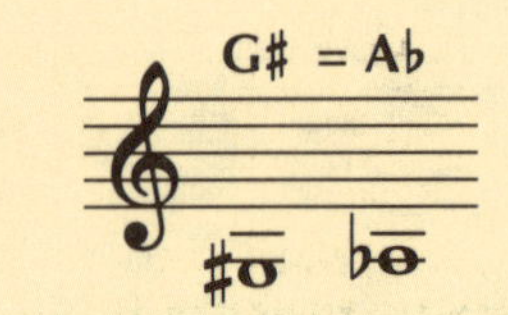

38 WARM-UP - Band Arrangement

39 E MINOR SCALE SKILL (Concert D Minor)

▶ Try playing both octaves.

40 TECHNIQUE BREAK

▶ * Use the alternate F♯ fingering.

41 FOR CLARINETS ONLY

SIXTEENTH REST

𝄿 = ¼ count in 2/4, 3/4, and 4/4 time.

A sixteenth rest is as long as a sixteenth note.

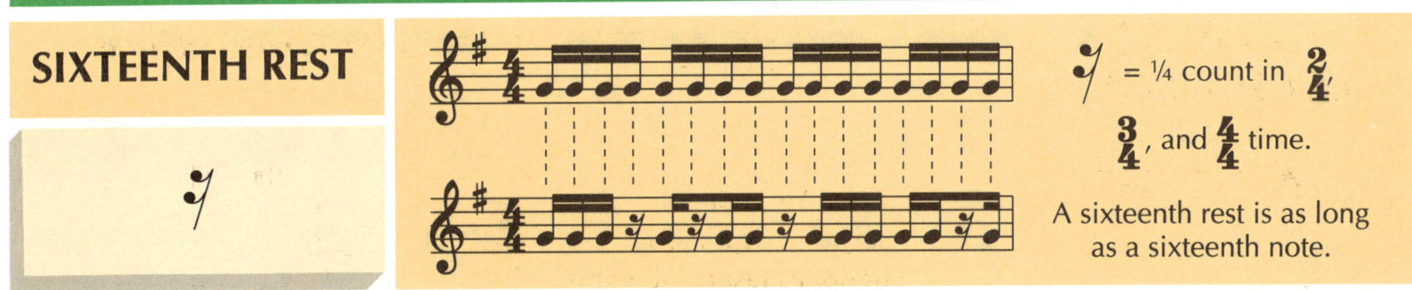

42 TINGA LAYO

Page 44

West Indies Folk Song

Moderato

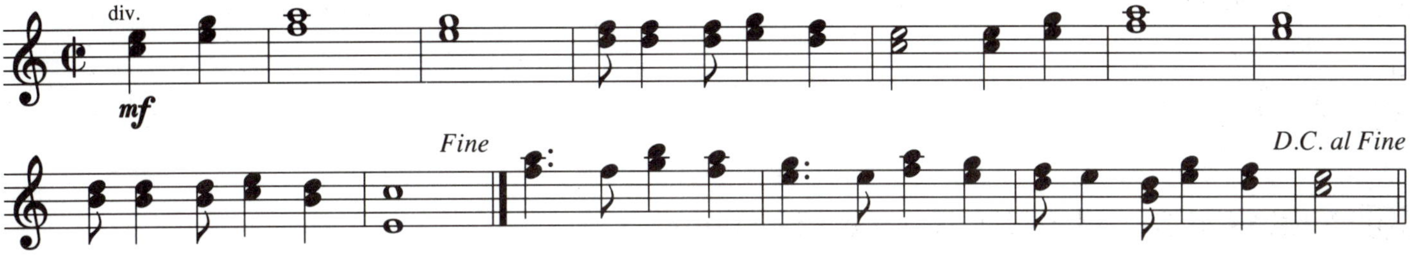
div.
mf
Fine
D.C. al Fine

43 HWI NE YA HE

American Indian Song

Allegro

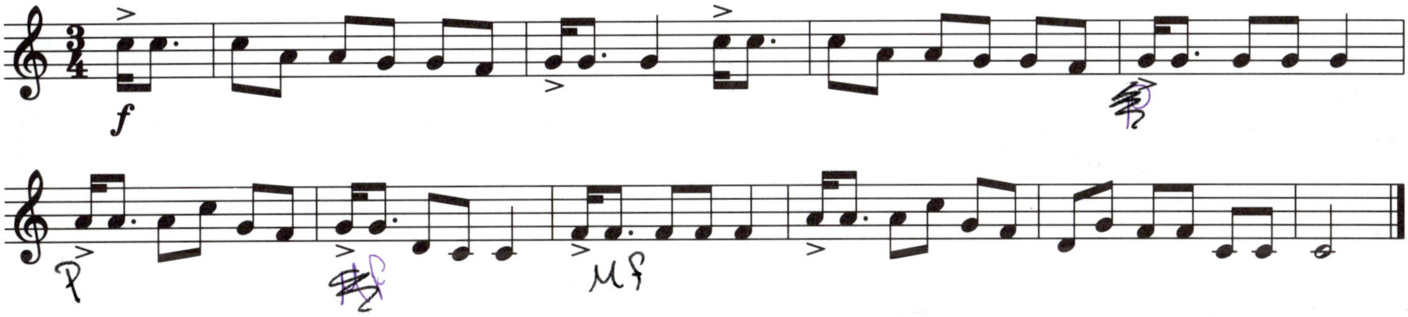
f

44 SIXTEENTH STUDY

Andantino

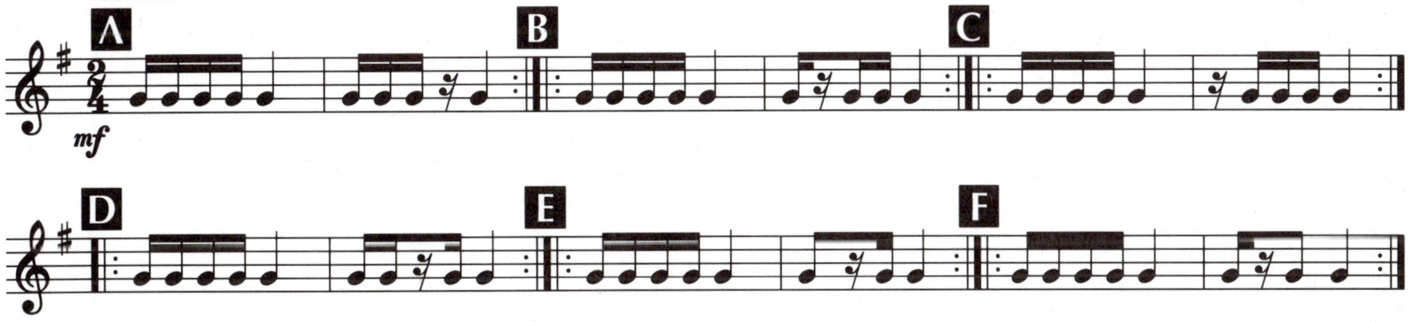
A
B
C
mf
D
E
F

▶ Write in the counting and clap the rhythm before you play.

45 GO FOR EXCELLENCE!

French Canadian Folk Song

Allegretto

"Envoyons D'L'Avant, Nos Gens!"

mp

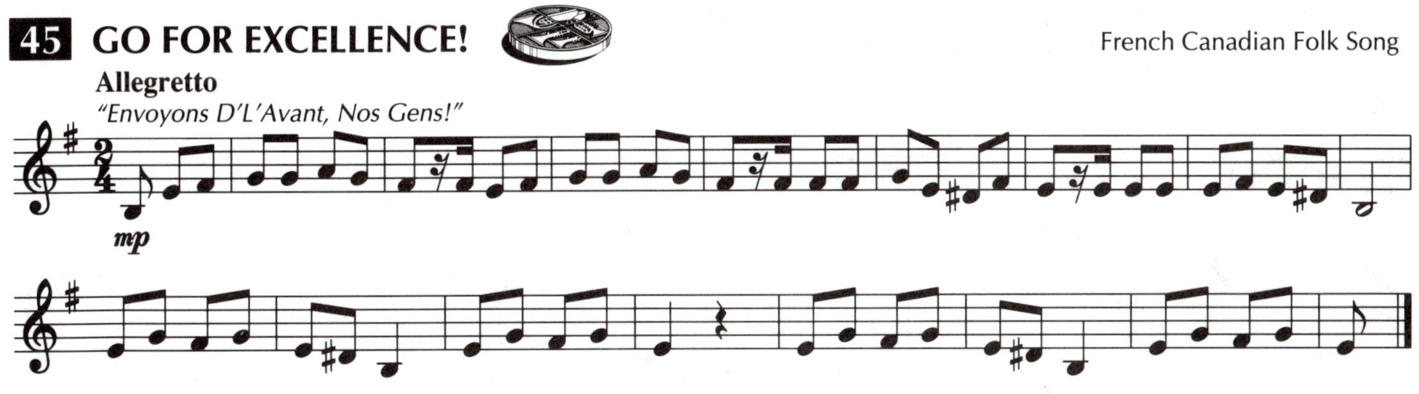

▶ Name the key in "Go For Excellence!"______________________

THE MIDDLE AGES (400 - 1400)

A dot after a rest adds half the value of the rest.

46 CONFIRMA HOC

Plainsong

▶ Keep the eighth notes even at all times.

47 DESCENDIT DE COELIS

Notre Dame Organum

48 ESTAMPIE

Anonymous

49 SUMER IS ICUMEN IN

English Round

THE RENAISSANCE (1400 - 1600)

E♭ MAJOR KEY SIGNATURE

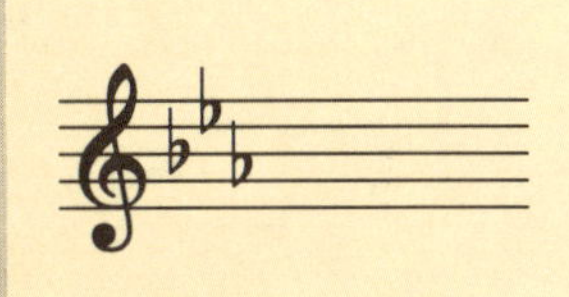

This key signature means play all B's as B flats, all E's as E flats, and all A's as A flats.

50 E♭ MAJOR SCALE SKILL (Concert D♭ Major)

▶ Try playing both octaves.

51 VOX DILECTI MEI - Band Arrangement

Palestrina (1525 - 1594)
arr. Bruce Pearson (b. 1942)

52 TECHNIQUE BREAK

53 GO FOR EXCELLENCE!

Thoinot Arbeau (1520 - 1595)

"The Official Branle"

58 FOR CLARINETS ONLY

Page 44

Eb
alternate
Andante
mf

▶ * Use the alternate Eb fingering.

EARLE OF OXFORDS MARCHE

Band Arrangement

William Byrd (1543 - 1623)
arr. Bruce Pearson (b. 1942)

Maestoso 4 · div. · *p* · *mp* · *mf* · *f* · *mp* · *ff* · 1. · 2. · *mf* · *rit.*

59

Arranger ______________ your name

Allegretto

▶ Create fauxbourdon by writing a duet part a sixth below this Renaissance melody. Title your composition, and play the top part while a friend plays the bottom part.

60 GO FOR EXCELLENCE!

Moderato

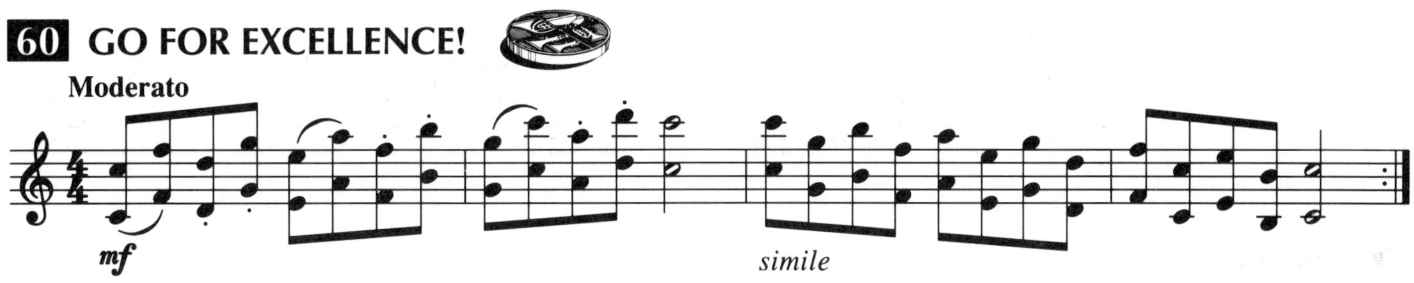

▶ Try playing both octaves.

THE BAROQUE PERIOD (1600 - 1750)

TRILL

A rapid alternation from the written note to the note above it in the key of the piece.

61 BALANCE BUILDER

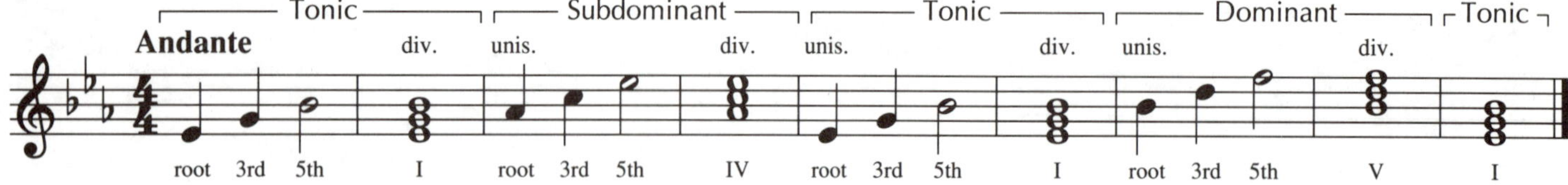

62 TRUMPET TUNE

Henry Purcell (1659 - 1695)

63 LE PETIT RIEN

François Couperin (1668 - 1733)

▶ When you see a staccato note at the end of a slur, slur to the note but make it short.

64 FOR CLARINETS ONLY  Page 44

▶ On the trills, move the key(s) as rapidly as possible. Keep the air moving.
▶ For your reference, a trill fingering chart is provided on page 47.

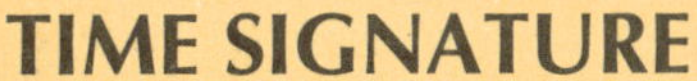

TIME SIGNATURE	9/8	**9** = 9 counts in each measure **8** = eighth note gets 1 count
STYLE		*grazioso* - gracefully

65 TECHNIQUE BREAK

Allegretto

mf
grazioso

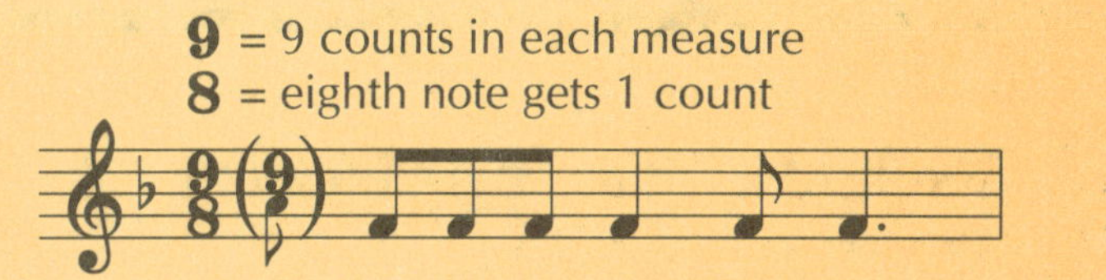

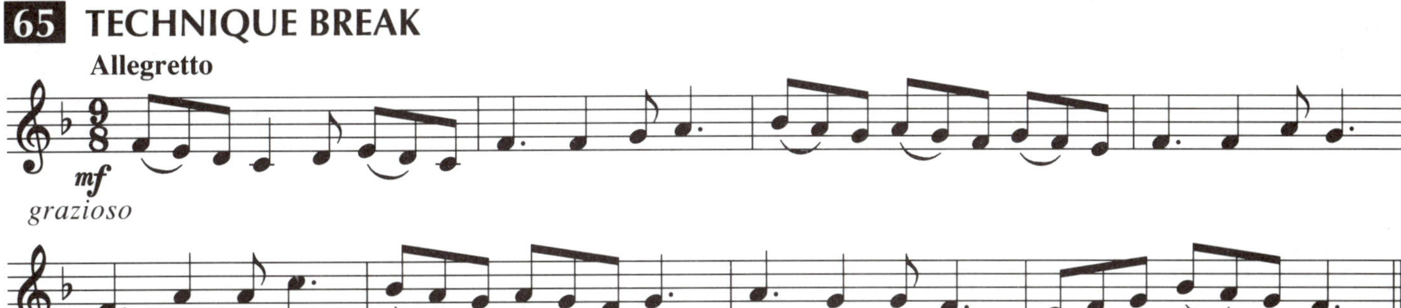

▶ Write in the counting and clap the rhythm before you play.

66 ALLEMANDE

Arcangelo Corelli (1653 - 1713)

Moderato

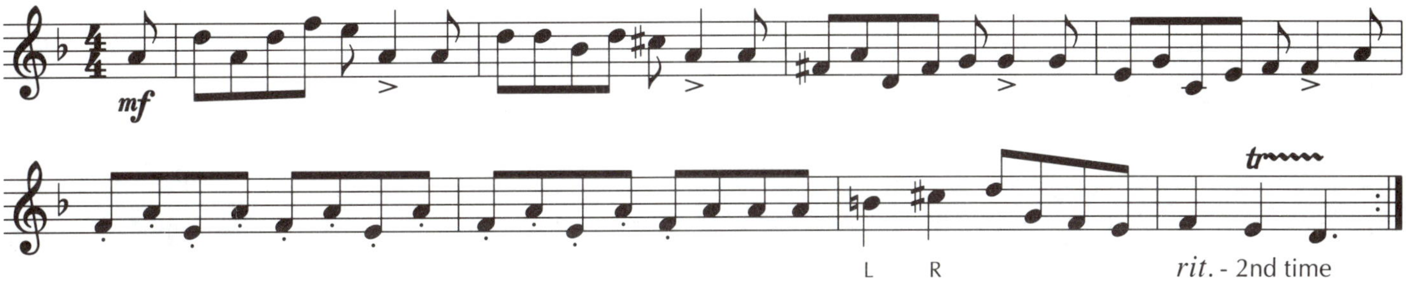

mf
L
R
rit. - 2nd time

67 THE FOUR SEASONS

Antonio Vivaldi (1678 - 1741)

Moderato

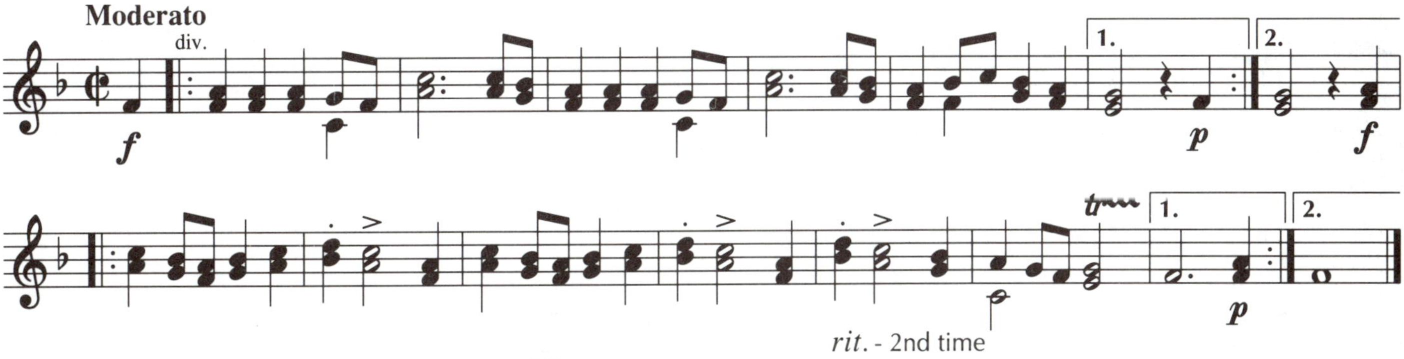

div.
f
1.
2.
p
f
rit. - 2nd time

68 GO FOR EXCELLENCE!

Johann Sebastian Bach (1685 - 1750)

Moderato

"Jesu, Joy of Man's Desiring"

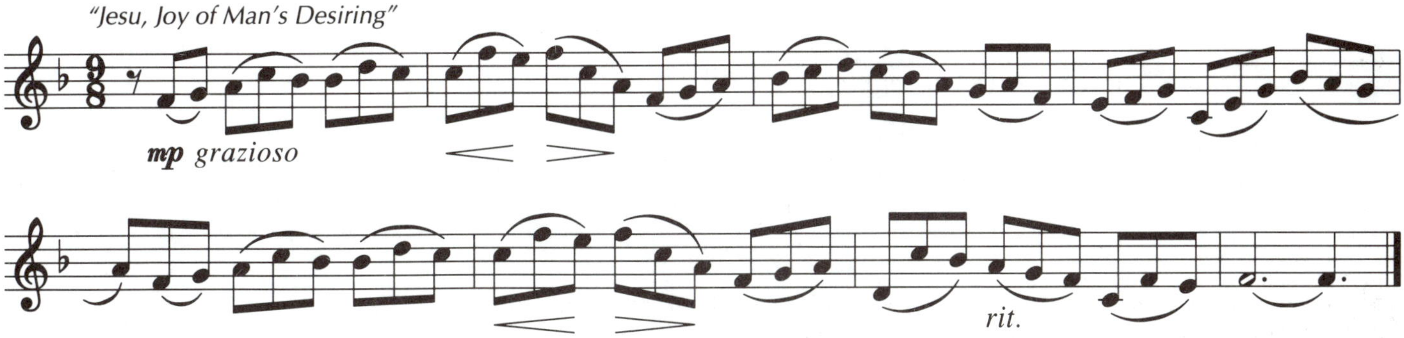

mp grazioso
rit.

69 CHORALE - Band Arrangement
Hans Leo Hassler (c. 1562 - 1612)
arr. Bruce Pearson (b. 1942)
Moderato
div.
p legato
1.
2.
70 HORNPIPE FROM "WATER MUSIC SUITE"
George Frideric Handel (1685 - 1759)
Maestoso
f
tr
1.
2.
71 TECHNIQUE BREAK
Andante
mf
1.
2.
72 FANTASIA CHROMATICA
Johann Sebastian Bach (1685 - 1750)
Moderato
mf
73 FOR CLARINETS ONLY
Page 44
E
L
B
L
A
Moderato
mf
L
B
Moderato
mf
L

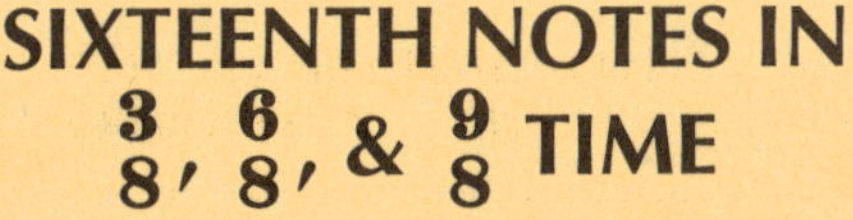

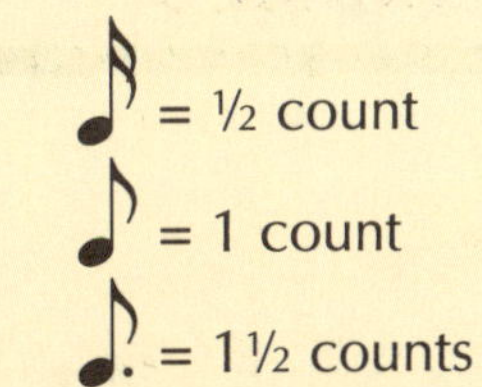

A single sixteenth note is half as long as an eighth note.

74 ARTICULATION ADVENTURE

Moderato

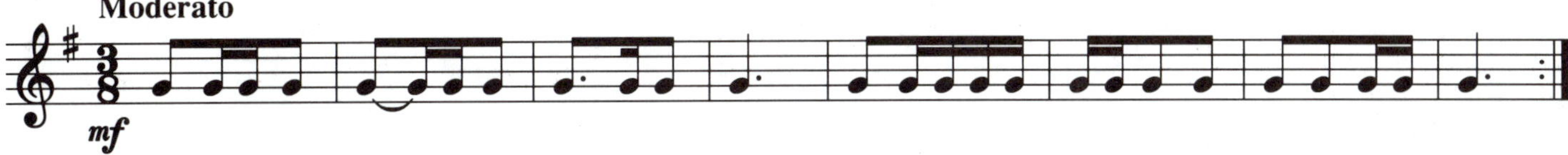

▶ Write in the counting and clap the rhythm before you play.

75 MINUETTO

Domenico Scarlatti (1685 - 1757)

Allegretto

▶ *cresc.* (<) - gradually play louder. *decresc.* (>) - gradually play softer.

76 PASSEPIED

Georg Philipp Telemann (1681 - 1767)

Allegro

77 GO FOR EXCELLENCE!

George Frideric Handel (1685 - 1759)

Andantino

"Siciliana from Music for the Royal Fireworks"

78 TECHNIQUE BREAK

▶ Name the key in "Technique Break." ______________________

REJOUISSANCE

from Music for the Royal Fireworks

Band Arrangement

George Frideric Handel (1685 - 1759)
arr. Bruce Pearson (b. 1942)

Moderato 1-15 15 16 17 18 19 div. 20 *f*

21 22 23 24 25 26 27 28

29 30 31 32 33 34 *mf*

35 36 37 38 39 40 41 *p*

42 43 44 45 46

47 48 49 50 51 unis. 52 div. *f*

53 54 55 56 57

58 59 60 61 62 63 64 *rit.*

THE CLASSICAL PERIOD (1750-1820)

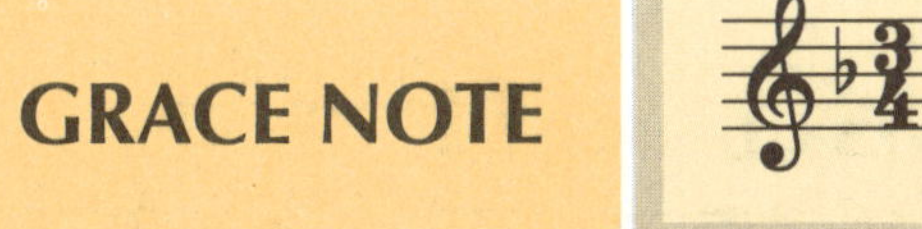

GRACE NOTE

A small-sized note played just before the note to which it is attached.

TEMPO

Larghetto - not as slow as **Largo**

STYLE

dolce - sweetly

79 THEME FROM PIANO SONATA NO. 2

Wolfgang Amadeus Mozart (1756 - 1791)

Larghetto

80 GERMAN DANCE

Franz Joseph Haydn (1732 - 1809)

Allegretto

81 TECHNIQUE BREAK

Moderato

82 GO FOR EXCELLENCE!

Ludwig van Beethoven (1770 - 1827)

Larghetto

"Sonatina"

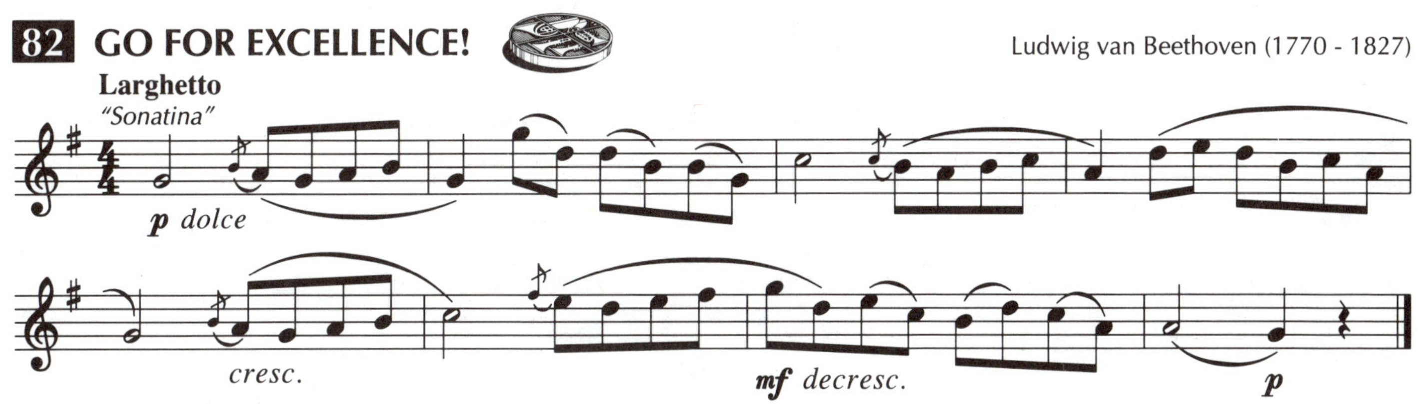

THE CLASSICAL PERIOD, continued

BINARY FORM — **AB** — Music that has two different sections.

ENHARMONICS

83 AUSTRIAN HYMN - Band Arrangement

Franz Joseph Haydn (1732 - 1809)
arr. Bruce Pearson (b. 1942)

84 RUSSIAN FOLK SONG

Ludwig van Beethoven (1770 - 1827)

85 TECHNIQUE BREAK

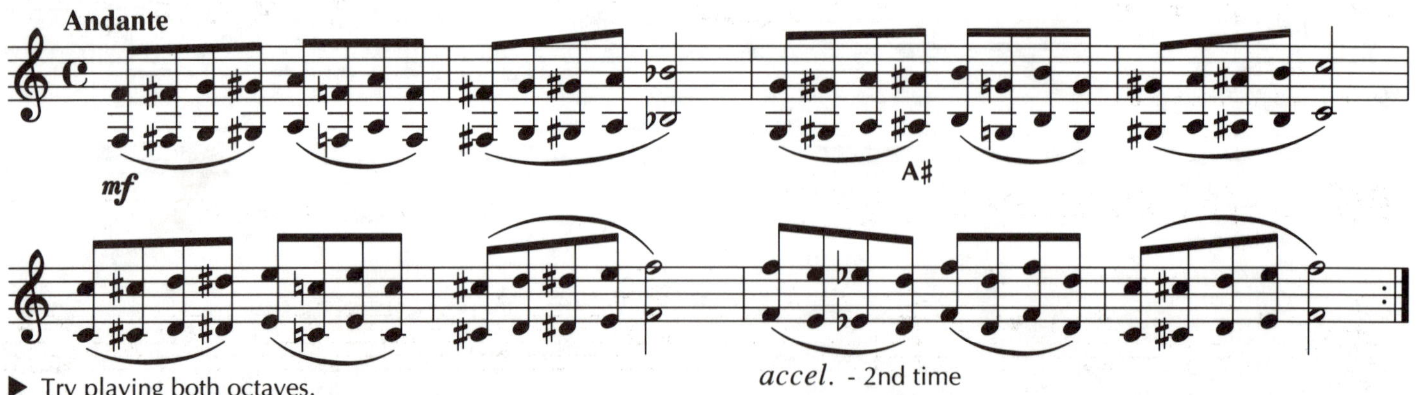

▶ Try playing both octaves.

86 FOR CLARINETS ONLY

Page 45

▶ Play each pattern four times. Start slowly and increase speed.

TERNARY FORM | **ABA** | The A section is followed by the B section, and then the A section is played again.

87 SCOTCH DANCE

Ludwig van Beethoven (1770 - 1827)

▶ * Use the alternate B fingering.
▶ Name the form used in "Scotch Dance." ______________________

88 TECHNIQUE BREAK

Rodolphe Kreutzer (1766 - 1831)

▶ Try playing both octaves.

89 GO FOR EXCELLENCE!

Wolfgang Amadeus Mozart (1756 - 1791)

RONDO FORM	ABACA	The main section A returns several times and alternates with other sections.

90 CADENCES

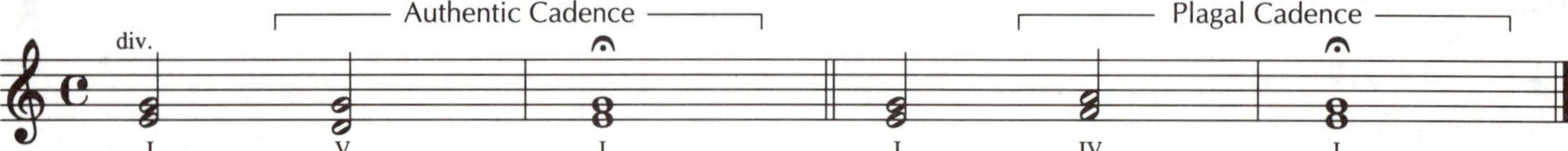

RONDO

Band Arrangement

Franz Joseph Haydn (1732 - 1809)
arr. Bruce Pearson (b. 1942)

A Section
Allegretto
div.
p mf p mf mp

9 B Section
p mf p mf f

17 A Section
p mf p mf

25 C Section
p mf p mf p mf p

33
unis. mf p
div.
unis. mf p
div.

41
f p

45 A Section
mf

48
p mf mp
1. 2.
mp

55
mf f

THE ROMANTIC PERIOD (1820 - 1900)

G MINOR KEY SIGNATURE

G minor has the same key signature as **B♭ major.**

91 CAST THY BURDEN FROM "ELIJAH" - Band Arrangement

Felix Mendelssohn (1809 - 1847)
arr. Bruce Pearson (b. 1942)

Largo

div.

pp *legato* *mp* *pp* *mf*

p *pp* *cresc.* *ff* *p*

92 G MINOR SCALE SKILL (Concert F Minor)

Page 45

Moderato

Natural Minor *mf* Harmonic Minor

Melodic Minor Arpeggio Chords div.

▶ Try playing both octaves.

93 TECHNIQUE BREAK

Moderato

mf

Fine

D. C. al Fine

94 GO FOR EXCELLENCE!

Johannes Brahms (1833 - 1897)

Allegretto

"Hungarian Dance No. 5"

f

THE ROMANTIC PERIOD, continued

TIME SIGNATURE	**6/4**	**6** = 6 counts in each measure **4** = quarter note gets 1 count
DAL SEGNO AL CODA (D.S. AL CODA)		Go back to the segno sign (𝄋) and play until the coda sign. When you reach the coda sign, skip to the ***Coda.***

95 SCHEHERAZADE

Nicolai Rimsky-Korsakov (1844 - 1908)

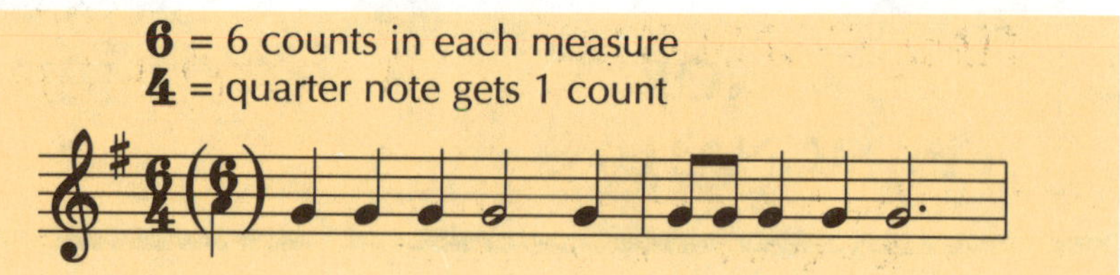

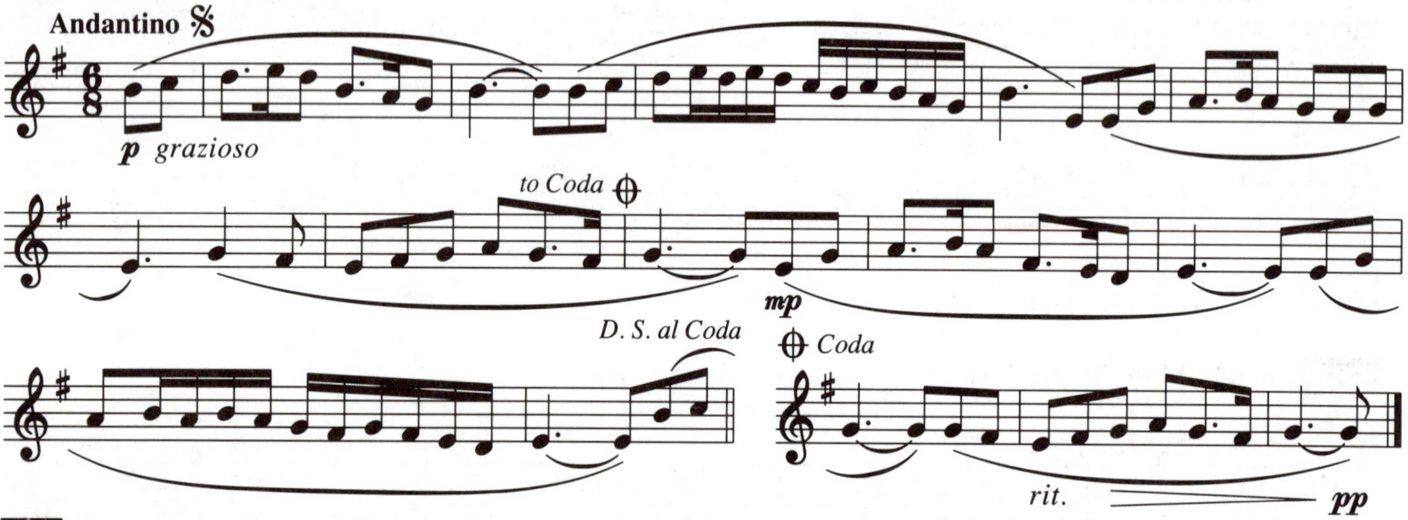

Andantino 𝄋
p grazioso
to Coda 𝄌
mp
D. S. al Coda
𝄌 *Coda*
rit.
pp

96 LAUGHING SONG FROM "DIE FLEDERMAUS"

Johann Strauss, Jr. (1825 - 1899)

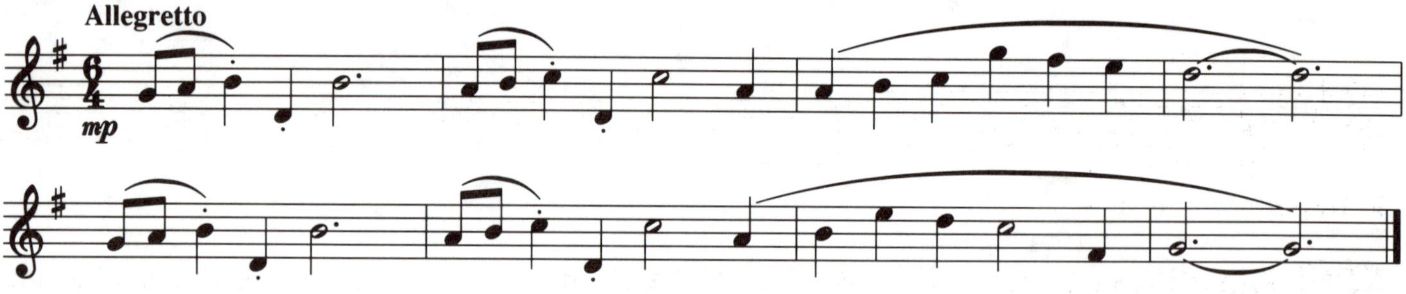

Allegretto
mp

▶ Write in the counting and clap the rhythm before you play.

97 FIRE FESTIVAL POLKA

Josef Strauss (1827 - 1870)

Moderato
f
p
1.
2.
mf
f

98 FOR CLARINETS ONLY

Page 45

F♯=G♭
R R

A
Moderato
mf
R L R
B
G♭
R
L

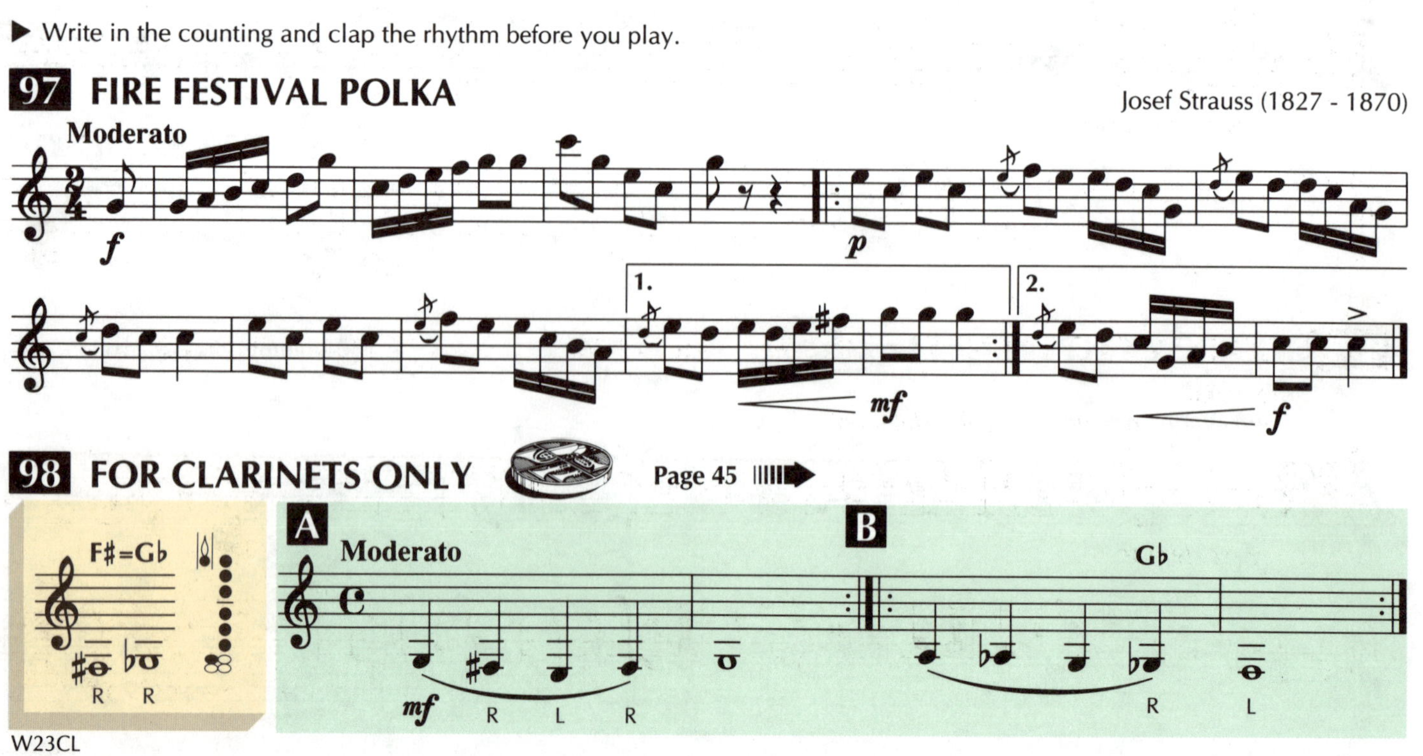

TIME SIGNATURE 5/4

5 = 5 counts in each measure
4 = quarter note gets 1 count

A MAJOR KEY SIGNATURE

This key signature means play all F's as F sharps, all C's as C sharps, and all G's as G sharps.

STYLE

sostenuto - sustained

99 TECHNIQUE BREAK

▶ Write in the counting and clap the rhythm before you play.

100 A MAJOR SCALE SKILL (Concert G Major)

▶ Try playing both octaves.

101 PILGRIMS CHORUS FROM "TANNHAUSER"

Richard Wagner (1813 - 1883)

102 GO FOR EXCELLENCE!

Page 45

Modeste Mussorgsky (1839 - 1881)

THE ROMANTIC PERIOD, continued

DYNAMICS

sforzando (sfz) - accented

103 ARTICULATION ADVENTURE

▶ Write in the counting and clap the rhythm before you play.

104 TECHNIQUE BREAK

Carl Czerny (1791 - 1857)

105 THE WILD HORSEMAN

Robert Schumann (1810 - 1856)

▶ Line A is in the key of A minor (concert G minor). On line B, write in the melody a whole step lower to transpose to the key of G minor (concert F minor). Play both lines.

106 FOR CLARINETS ONLY

STYLE | ***cantabile*** - in a singing style

WALTZ

from Waltz Op. 39, No. 15

Band Arrangement

Johannes Brahms (1833 - 1897)
arr. Chris Salerno (b. 1968)

1-7 **Moderato** 7 | 8 | 9 | 10 | 11 div.

f cantabile

12 unis. | 13 | 14 | 15 | 16 | 17 | 18 div.

p cresc.

19 | 20 | 21 | 22 | 23 unis. | 24 div.

f

25 | 26 unis. | 27 | 28 | 29 | 30 div.

rit.

107 TECHNIQUE BREAK

Moderato

C or ¢

mf *simile*

- * Use the alternate F♯/G♭ and B fingerings.
- Try playing both octaves.

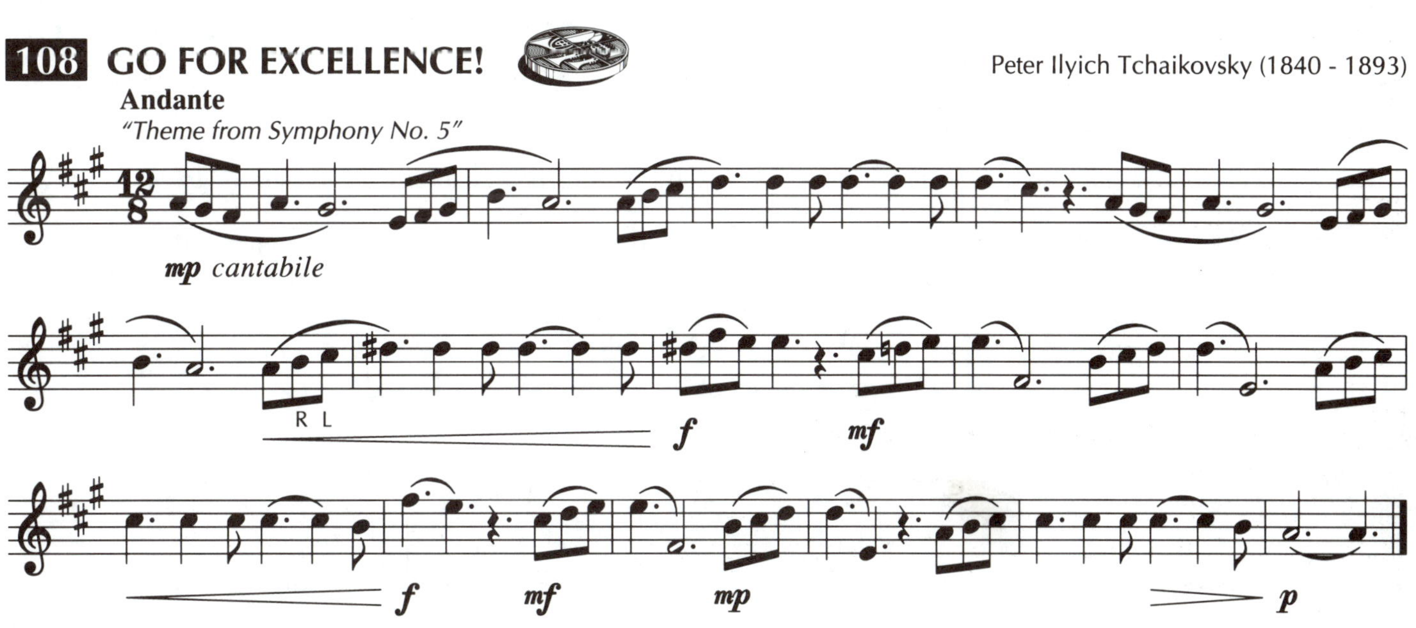

B MINOR KEY SIGNATURE

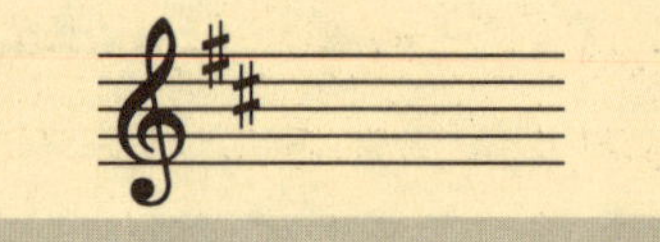

B minor has the same key signature as **D major.**

109 B MINOR SCALE SKILL (Concert A Minor)

Page 45

▶ Try playing both octaves.

110 PAVANE

Gabriel Fauré (1845 - 1924)

111 WHOLE-TONE SCALE STUDY

▶ A whole-tone scale consists of only whole steps.

112 EXCERPT FROM "PRELUDE TO THE AFTERNOON OF A FAUN"

Impressionism Example
Claude Debussy (1862 - 1918)

▶ This piece is based on a whole-tone scale. In measure 6, be sure to trill up a whole step. Use the trill fingering found on p. 47.

113 THE SUNKEN CATHEDRAL - Band Arrangement

Impressionism Example
Claude Debussy (1862 - 1918)
arr. Chuck Elledge (b. 1961)

▶ This piece demonstrates a technique called planing, where all notes of a chord move the same direction. This is also called parallel motion.

ASYMMETRICAL METERS

Meters or time signatures with an uneven number of eighth notes (usually 3/8, 5/8, or 7/8).

114 FOLK MELODY A LA BÉLA BARTÓK (1881 - 1945)

Nationalism Example
Stephen Foster (1826 - 1864)
arr. Chris Salerno (b. 1968)

Allegretto
"Oh! Susanna"

115 ODE TO IGOR STRAVINSKY (1882 - 1971) - Band Arrangement

Page 46

Primitivism Example
Chris Salerno (b. 1968)

Moderato

116 TECHNIQUE BREAK

▶ Write in the counting and clap the rhythm before you play.

117 GO FOR EXCELLENCE!

Claude Debussy (1862 - 1918)

Allegro
"Golliwog's Cake Walk from Children's Corner"

DYNAMICS	*forte-piano* (*fp*) - loud, then immediately soft

118 HOMAGE TO ANTON WEBERN (1883 - 1945)

Twelve-tone Example
Chris Salerno (b. 1968)

▶ Notice that the tone row uses all twelve notes of the chromatic scale once.

119 TONE ROW

Page 46

120

Composer ______________________
your name

▶ Compose a twelve-tone composition. Title and play your composition.

121 FOR CLARINETS ONLY

WAR
from The Four Horsemen
Band Arrangement

▶ Write in the counting and clap the rhythm before you play.

STYLE

Swing - played as

TWO-MEASURE REPEAT SIGN

Repeat the two previous measures.

128 SWINGING BLUES SCALE

129 SWINGING BLUES CHORD PROGRESSION (Arpeggios)

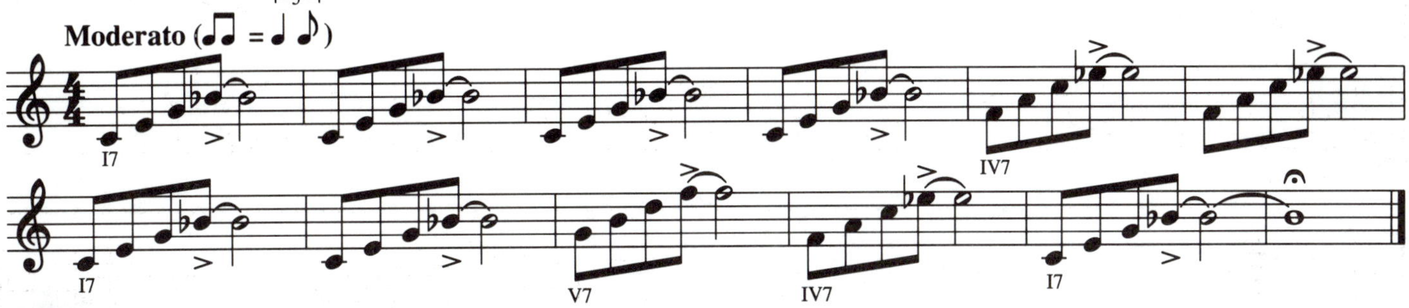

130 BLUES CHORD ACCOMPANIMENT - Band Arrangement

▶ This exercise can be played with 131 and 132.

131 TIN ROOF BLUES

Page 46

Traditional Blues Example

132 GO FOR EXCELLENCE!

▶ Write in the counting and clap the rhythm before you play.

JAMBALAYA JAMMIN'

Band Arrangement

James "Red" McLeod (b. 1912)

SCALE STUDIES

1 C MAJOR SCALE (Concert B♭ Major)

2 A HARMONIC MINOR SCALE (Concert G Harmonic Minor)

3 F MAJOR SCALE (Concert E♭ Major)

4 D HARMONIC MINOR SCALE (Concert C Harmonic Minor)

Scale Studies

5 G MAJOR SCALE (Concert F Major)

6 E HARMONIC MINOR SCALE (Concert D Harmonic Minor)

7 B♭ MAJOR SCALE (Concert A♭ Major)

8 G HARMONIC MINOR SCALE (Concert F Harmonic Minor)

SCALE STUDIES

9 D MAJOR SCALE (Concert C Major)

10 B HARMONIC MINOR SCALE (Concert A Harmonic Minor)

11 E♭ MAJOR SCALE (Concert D♭ Major)

12 A MAJOR SCALE (Concert G Major)

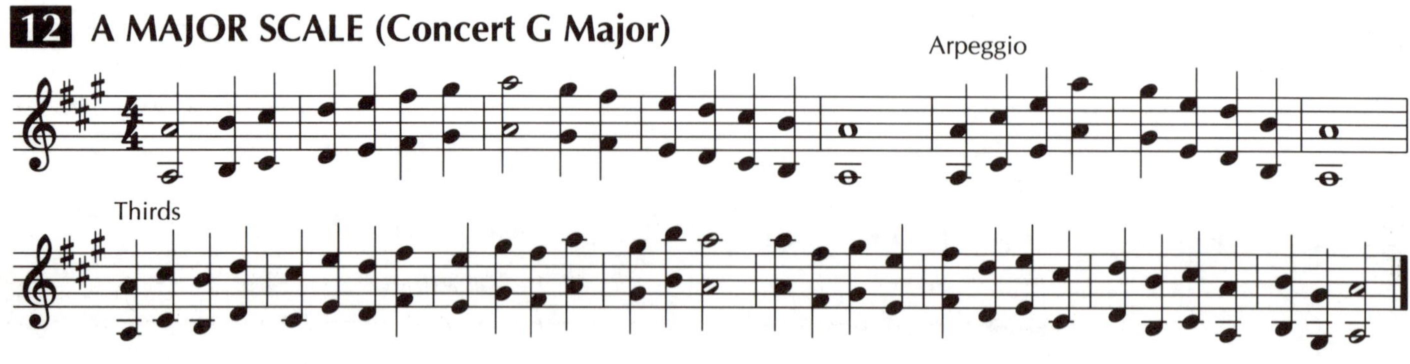

13 CHROMATIC SCALE

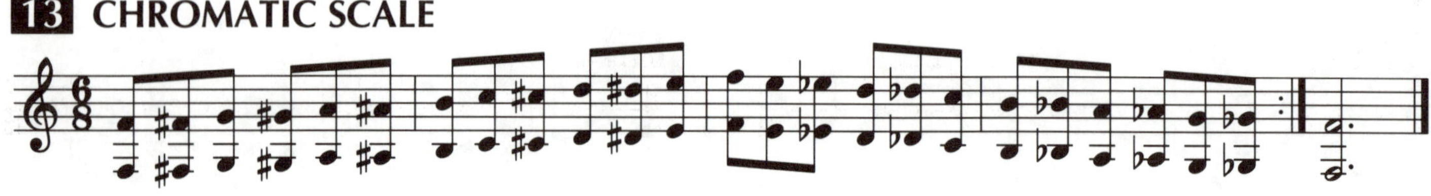

RHYTHM STUDIES

2/4

1

2

3

4

5

6

7

8

3/4

1

2

3

4

5

6

7

8

9

3 3 3 3

10

RHYTHM STUDIES

RHYTHM STUDIES

EXCELLERATORS-FOR CLARINETS ONLY

EXCELLERATORS-For Clarinets Only

EXCELLERATORS-For Clarinets Only

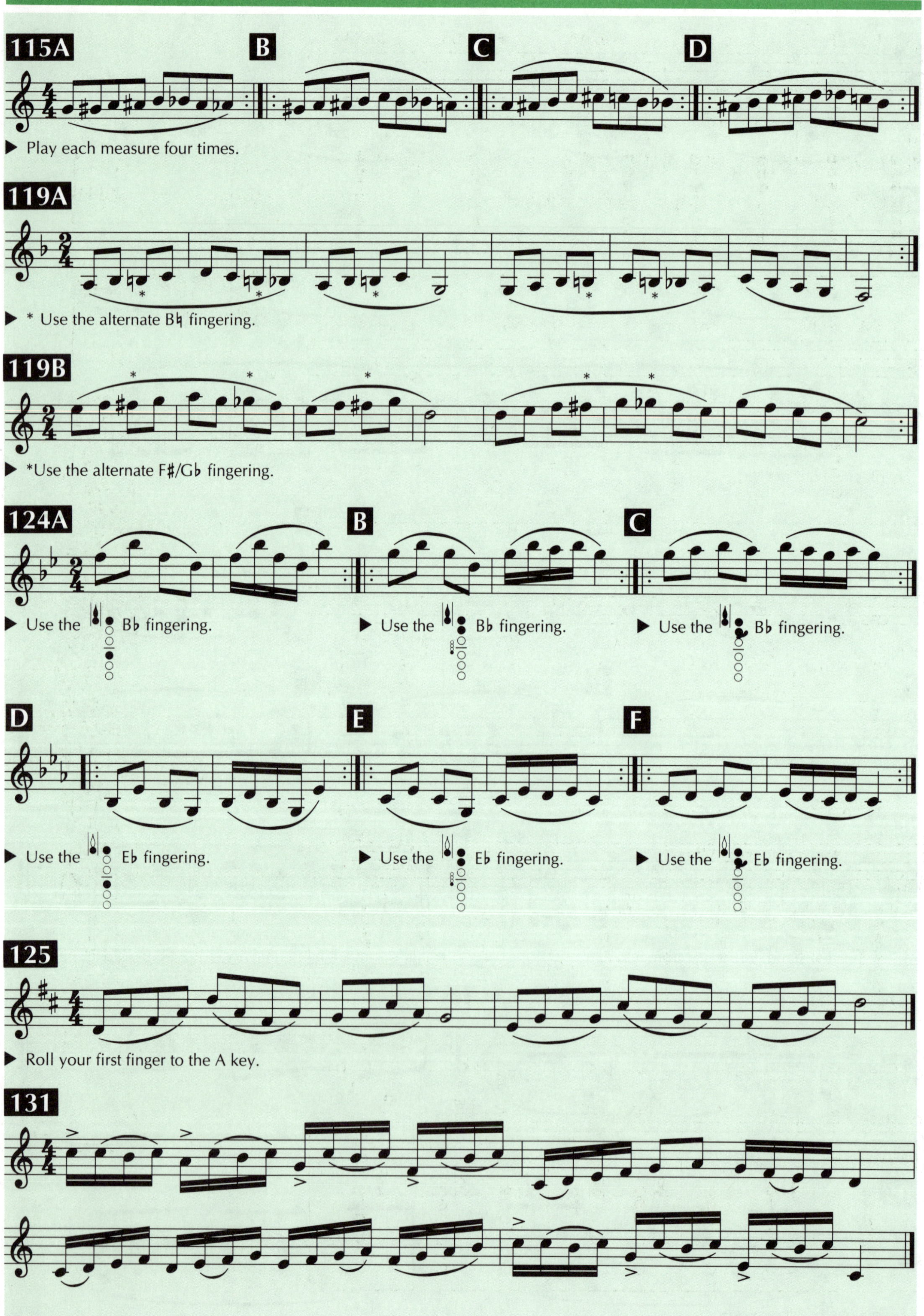

B♭ Clarinet Trill Fingering Chart

○ = open
● = pressed down

Move the red key rapidly to produce the trill.

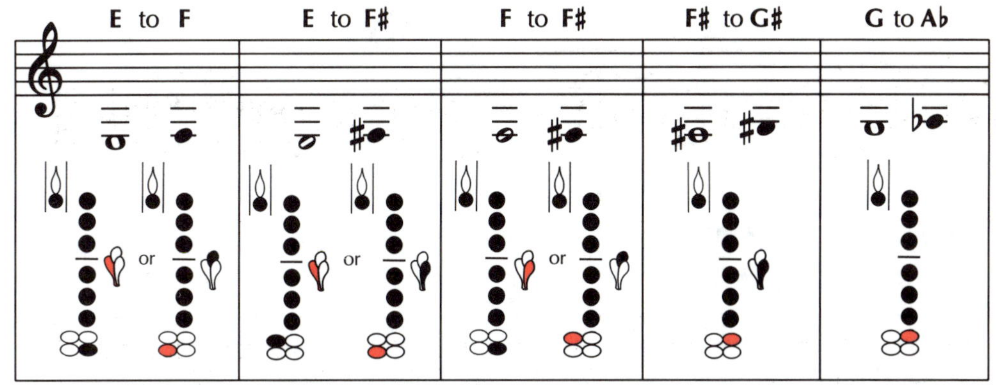

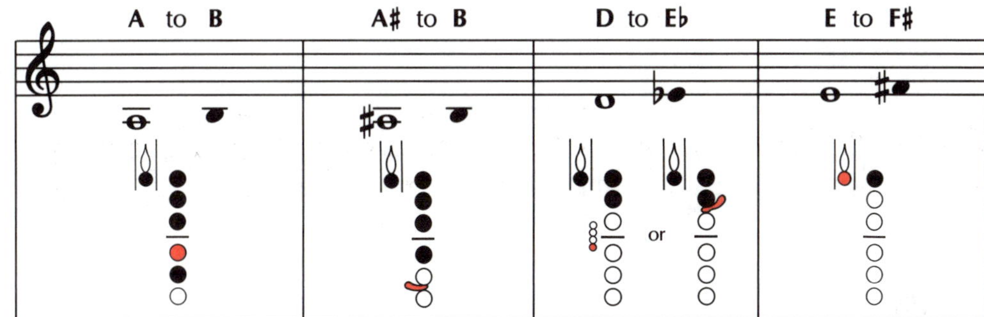

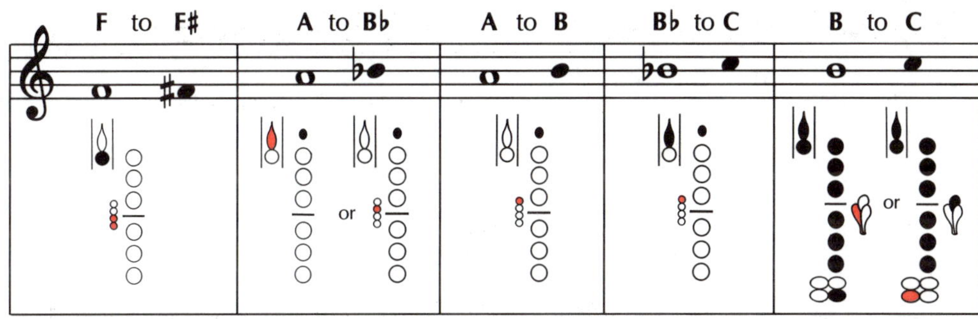

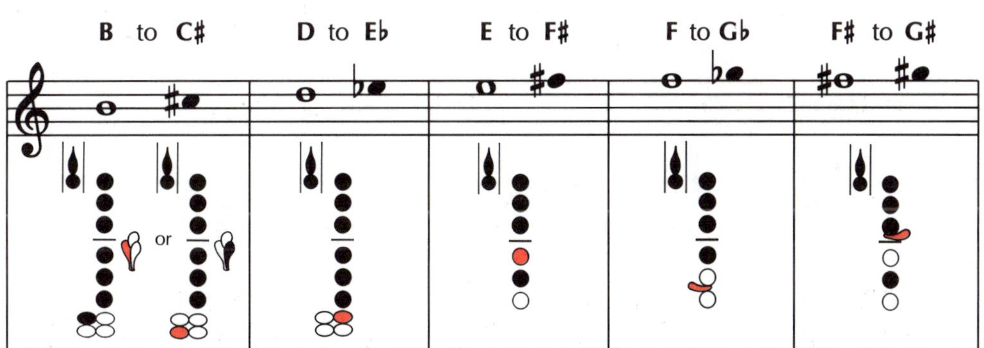

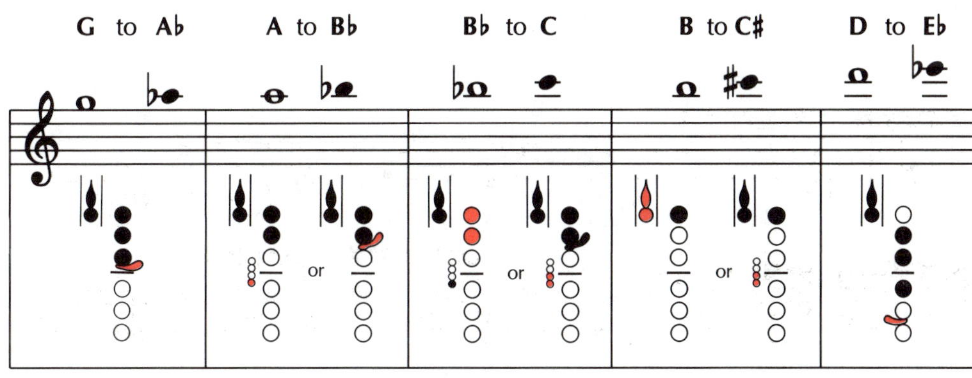

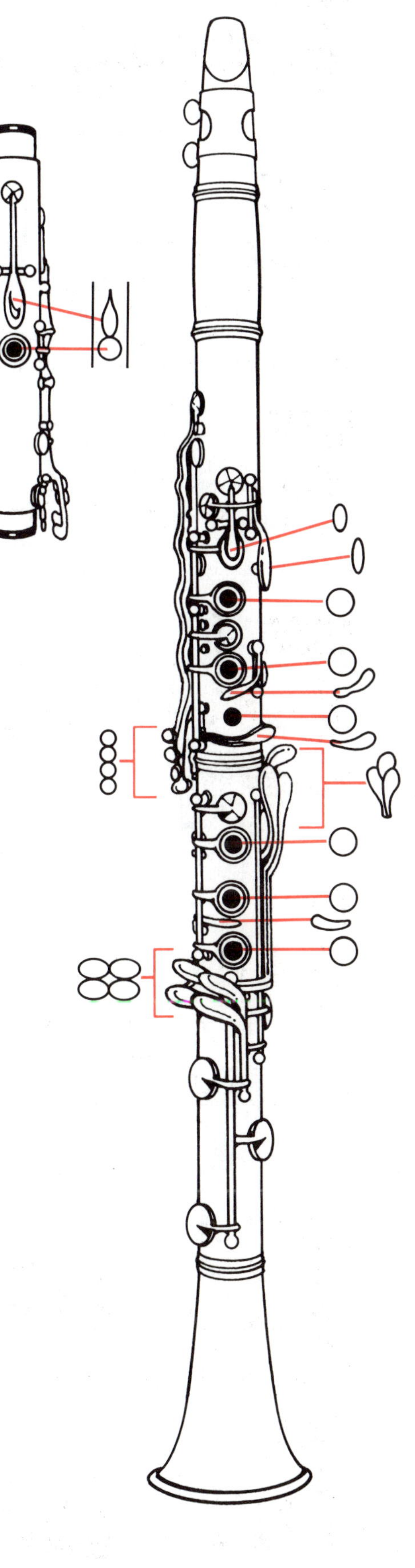

B♭ Clarinet Fingering Chart

○ = open
● = pressed down

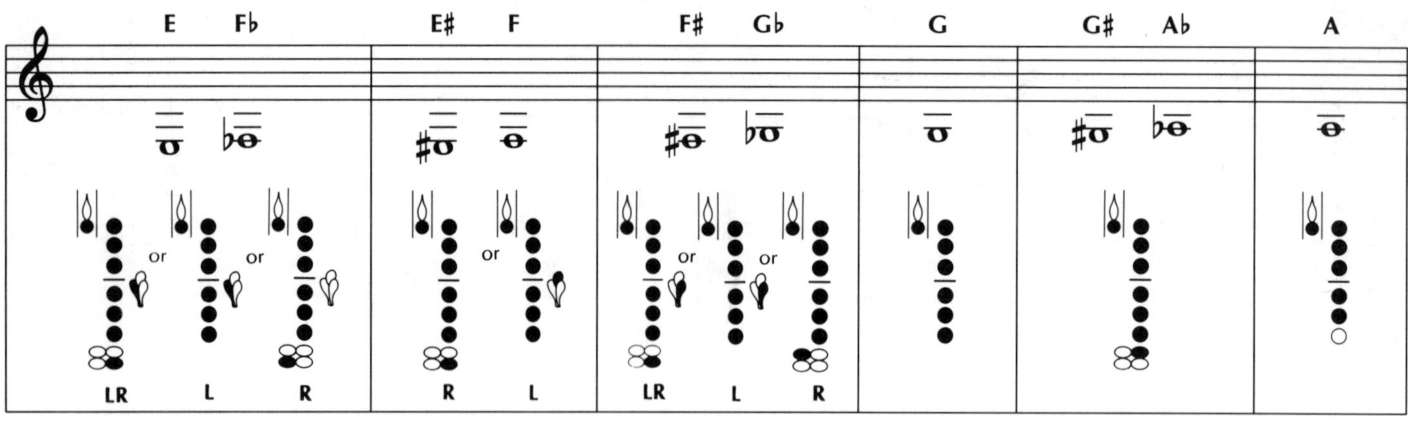

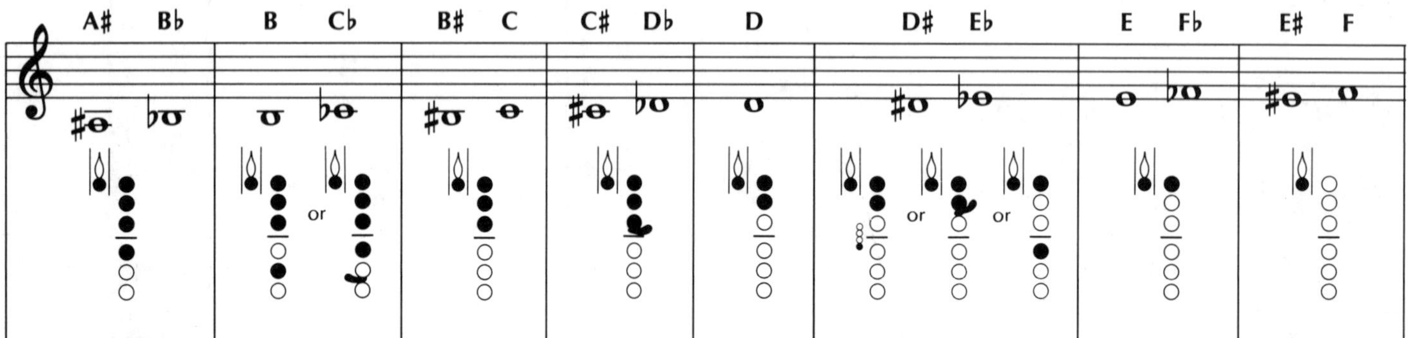

F♯ G♭ | G | G♯ A♭ | A | A♯ B♭ | B C♭ | B♯ C

or

LR L R | R L

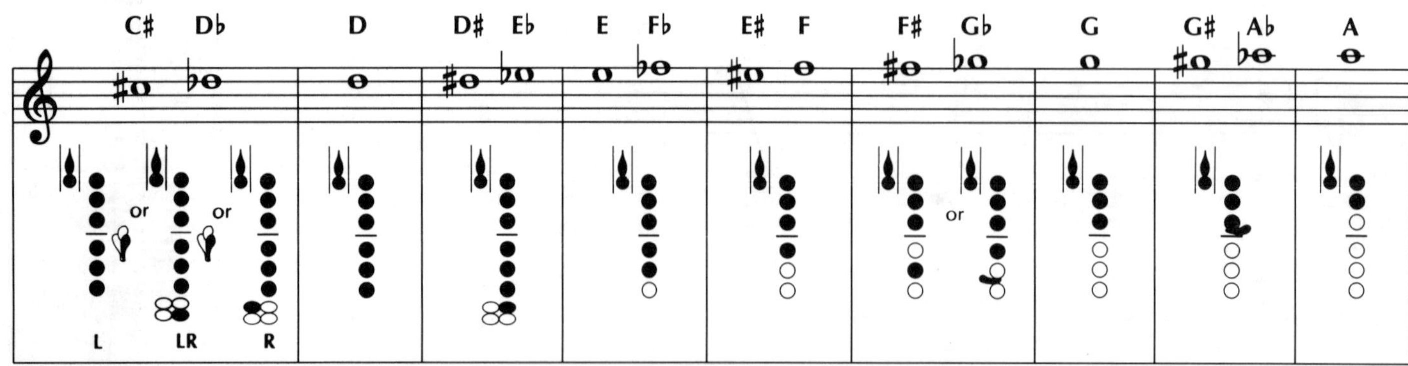

A♯ B♭ | B C♭ | B♯ C | C♯ D♭ | D | D♯ E♭ | E F♭ | F

or